By Centurion Publications, a division of Centurion Financial, LLC

I0463212

A Guide to Business Communication
Writing, Presenting, and Listening

ISBN 1-449-59706-8

EAN-13 9781449597061

A Guide to Business Communication

By

C Bracken Meyers

Contents

"Wise men talk because they have something to say; fools, because they have to say something."

-PLATO

Preface

Communication is the most valuable skill in the work place and can be considered a form of art. Good communication skills will help you go far in both your personal and professional life. Being able to successfully communicate in business is the most important qualification employers actively look for when hiring new staff.

Businesses strive to employ people who possess strong verbal and written skills, because business communications are an important component of having a successful business.

No matter what level of expertise in communications you are at, you can always improve. This book will serve you as a guide and reference to help you improve your communication skills.

C Bracken Meyers

This page is intentionally left blank

Section 1

Writing

Proper business communication is crucial to success of an organization or individual. Business writing is often the main line of communication inside and outside of any organization, making writing one of the most important skills to master.

Good communication helps to ensure an efficient operation of all levels within an organization. Poor communication is common, and often results in inefficiencies, leading to a loss of productivity and consequently, a loss of profits.

Set Your Writing Objective

In business writing your objective is always to convey a message. Before you begin to write, clearly define the message you need to convey in your mind or on a post-it note. Focus on that message, and then make it your goal to convey that message to reader. Make every word, every sentence, and every paragraph work towards accomplishing that one goal.

Write For the Reader

Many letters, memos, and reports are written from the perspective of the writer and not the reader. You might write the same message in many different ways, depending on who will be reading it. This can cause the message to be lost or misconstrued if you are not writing for your reader.

> If a document has to be read twice to understand the meaning, don't count on anyone getting the message.

Business correspondence must clearly convey the message to the reader on the first reading. The business world is too busy to study letters looking for obscure or hidden meanings.

Two questions you should ask yourself while writing:

1. Is the reader already going to know this information? – Try to eliminate any information that the reader will already know.

2. What message does this letter convey? – If the letter does not fully convey your objective, you need to do some rewriting.

Get Into Your Readers Mind

A company specializing in the manufacturing of small children's toys may require its engineers to spend time crawling around on the floor. This will help give the development team the same perspective as a child, the user of the product. If they can look at the toy in the same point of view of the user, they will have a better chance of success. The same is true if you can get into your reader's mind frame. If you know what they need to know, you can write a letter that conveys the appropriate information in the best form possible.

> TIP: Before you start to write that important business letter, ask yourself this question, "Who is this letter for? What do I want them to do after reading it?" Visualize the reader and then begin to write. This will give you a better chance of getting your message across.

Write So Your Reader Can Understand

Jargon is terminology which is especially defined in relationship to a specific activity, profession, or group. Jargon can be a set of words, phrases, truncated terminologies, or acronyms, in which the meaning is known only within a particular group. Jargon can make communicating easier within that specific group, but it may appear like alien language to others. Think of jargon as a kind of shorthand, which makes it an effective way to communicate with members of that specific group.

Usually jargon does not have any alternatives that make it easy for outsiders to understand. Here are a few examples:

> A large barrier in business correspondence is the inappropriate use of jargon.

Laparoscopy – is a medical term referring to the process in which a surgeon uses a special probing technique to investigate anomalies inside your internal organs with the aid of a computer.

30 lb duplex – refers to a type of paper that frequently flies around in the conversations of publishing and the printing industry.

GAAP – Generally Accepted Accounting Principles, is the finance industry's lingo which refers to the standard set of rules for financial accounting.

There is another problem with using jargon with outsiders. Sometimes you might use a jargon term that might have a different meaning in different industries. This is most common with acronyms. A common one I have found is 'IP.' To a computer technician, this means 'internet protocol,' to a patent attorney, this means 'intellectual property.'

This is why you need to be careful while writing to individuals outside your industry. When you find yourself using an uncommon phrase or term, ask yourself if your reader will be able to understand it. If not, find a way to say it in plain language.

Focus on What Your Reader Needs to Know

Imagine your boss just asked you to prepare a report on a new market segment, and make a recommendation if the company should enter into that market. After researching and compiling all the information needed, you begin writing the report:

> First learn the meaning of what you say, and then speak."- Epictetus

"You asked me to prepare a report on the market demand for tech-widgets, what they are, possible manufacturers, and geographic sales estimates."

Does this sound like an effective first paragraph? Is it grabbing your attention? Many reports start off this way. You are writing to the person who asked you for the report, you do not need to tell them what they asked for, they already know. Reports should contain the answers to the questions and not the questions themselves. A reader's interest is at the greatest in the first few sentences. Your objective is to engage the reader's attention immediately. Here is a good example of the same report:

> "According to my research, there is a growing demand for tech-widgets, I recommend we enter this market quickly."

Focus only on what the reader needs to know, and discard any information the reader will already know. A good way to start is by thinking of the questions your reader might ask about your topic, and then let the answers form the basis of the report.

Writing Tone

It is important to know when to be formal or informal, when to be conciliatory, and how to make effective requests and demands. Although most business communications require a degree of formality, it is useful to know when to be friendly and how to make your writing reflect a friendly tone. Individual customers often respond well to writing which they feel is slightly more personal and less distant. It is wise to tailor the level of formality within your business communications to the individual client, whenever possible. If you are responding directly to a customer's letter, try to match the level of formality that the customer has used.

Many letters are sent everyday that are interpreted by the reader as unfriendly, although the writer did not intend them to be so. These letters are using a negative written tone. When communicating verbally, it is easy to tell when someone is being polite or sarcastic by the tone of their voice. In writing, tone is just as important as it is in speech, but because the other person cannot hear the actual tone of our words, our writing must clearly convey our tone by the choice of the words we use and in the order in which we use them.

There are two types of word tones, positive and negative. When we use positive words, people will automatically set up a positive mind frame, and their response is likely to also be positive. Using negative words is likely to invoke a negative response.

> "Seek first to understand, then to be understood"
> - Stephen Covey

If I said to you, "Hannah did not attend the conference," what would you think? You would probably take it at face value that Hannah was not at

5

the conference. However, if I said instead, "Hannah failed to attend the conference," wouldn't that change your perspective? That suggests that she should have been there, and the fact that she was not, implies a failure of some kind.

The following two groups of words will help depict the difference between written negative and positive word tones:

Negative:

fault | failure | blame | inferior | negligence | penalty

Positive:

please | thank you | understand | agree | appreciate

Here is an example paragraph that makes use of negative words:

"Having just received your complaint regarding our tech-widget, I must say I completely fail to understand why you should be confused. We enclosed an instructional manual with the product, which has been compiled by technically competent personnel. This manual should be readily understood by anyone that can understand a six grade reading level. We have received no other complaints, and so I must conclude we are not at fault and cannot agree to your demand for a refund."

Here is the same paragraph stuffed with positive words:

"I am sorry you had a problem with the manual for our tech-widget. Although we have done our best to make our manual user friendly, using tech-widgets can still be confusing. So that you won't miss out on the benefits of the great new product, I would like to speak to you over the phone and try to answer any of your questions. Please call me any time this week, and if this is acceptable to you we can talk through the process together. I very much want to be of assistance to you and look forward to your call."

Out of these two examples, which one would be more likely to retain a valuable customer?

Use Simple Words

Simple words help to convey your message. Professionals regularly have a problem with using too many complex words. They are afraid people will think of them as uneducated, however, this is not true. If you use simple words, people will not notice them because they will be too busy receiving the message.

Here are a few examples of simple words you can substitute for complex ones:

Locate → Find   **Optimum → Best**

Furnish → Provide   **Forward → Send**

Terminate → Stop   **Concept → Idea**

This does not mean that you cannot ever use complex words. Just try to eliminate them wherever possible. It is harder to read something that uses several complex words in a single sentence, which creates a barrier to communication.

> When there is a choice – and there almost always is – use the simpler word.

When writing in a highly formal style, writers sometimes use long words (usually Latin or French in origin) in order to try and make a good impression. There is nothing strictly wrong with this, but you should be wary of overreaching yourself. I have experienced hundreds of cases in which people have used long words in which they did not fully understand their meanings. Often this made them seem slightly ridiculous. In some cases, it led to them saying something completely different than what they intended to say.

Remember that there is no point in using impressive words if your readers are unable to understand the meaning of your message. In literary writing, it is reasonable to expect readers to have an interest in expanding their vocabularies;

> Sometimes people might be suspicious of documents which they feel may be using obscure language to try and hide unpleasant information.

however, this should not be the case in business writing. It is best to make business documents clear and simple.

When you have finished writing a document, read through it and use a dictionary to look up any words that you are not entirely certain about the meaning. If this seems strenuous, keep in mind that every time you look up a word you will learn something new, so there will be fewer words to look up in the future. If you want to expand your vocabulary further, the best way is to engage in recreational reading. When you read, you will learn about new words without even noticing it, and you will be able to write more confidently as a result.

Remove Fluff

There are two main kinds of writing fluff that you need to watch for, redundant words and extra words. Many letters, emails, and even informational books could be reduced in size by around 25% if you remove all the unnecessary words.

The key to removing extra words is simple, say everything as simply as possible. Do not use long or complex phrases, such as, "in the majority of instances," when you can just use "usually" instead. Another good example is "at this point in time," you can easily use "at present" or "now." Anytime you can use a single word instead of a phrase, go with the single word.

The other form of fluff is the redundant words. Here are a few good examples:

"This young man has a great future ahead of him." – Where else would his future be but ahead?

"Today a new breakthrough in motor science occurred…." – Would you ever say an old breakthrough? Just saying breakthrough is sufficient.

> When editing what you have written, look for instances where you have said the same thing twice, and take out the fluff.

"There has been an unexpected emergency at the office." – It is in the nature of an emergency to be unexpected.

Here are a few more examples of redundant word fluff:

1.   foreign import

2.   due and payable

3.   absolutely perfect

4.   necessary requisite

5.   10 a.m. in the morning.

6.   permission and approval

7.   the resulting consequence

Spelling and Grammar Matter

I would like to quickly cover some common errors found in business writing. If you find yourself having problems with grammar, then I recommend that you spend some time studying. There are many great books, online tutorials, and classes to help you improve your grammatical skills.

Proofreading

It is far too common to feel that it is unnecessary to pay a lot of attention to your spelling if you are using a computer with a spell checker. Spell checkers are far from perfect. They may not be familiar with trade-specific terminology that you might use. Even a well established spell checker will often fail to spot real words which have accidentally been written in place of other real words, such as, missing the 'm' off the end of 'form', would result in 'leave for' instead of 'leave form'. Most spell checkers have no understanding of context and will not fix this type of error.

The best way to use a spell checker is to combine it with manual proofreading and editing. Let spell check run through a document first, informing you when it thinks it has found mistakes. This will help you to get rid of a lot of small errors and will thus reduce the amount of time you need to spend proofreading the document.

Proofreading is a skill that must be learned, and with practice you will find that you notice errors more easily. You will also become more familiar with your common mistakes which will improve your accuracy in the future.

Homonyms, Apostrophes and the Right Word

Being aware of which homonyms to look out for is important when proofreading. Many people are not sure which of these common words are supposed to go where.

Frequently I see a mix up between 'eg' and 'i.e.'

'Eg' means 'for example.'

'I.e.' means 'in other words.' eg: "where I work best, i.e., the coffee shop."

Confusion often occurs between 'there,' 'their' and 'they're.'

'There' is used to describe a position, eg: "The car is over there."

'Their' means 'belonging to them.' "That is their car."

'They're' is an abbreviation for 'they are.' "They're looking for the car."

Many writers confuse 'to', 'too' and 'two.'

'To' is directional, eg: "I'm going to the office." Note that it can refer to time as well as space, eg: "I'm going to be late."

'Too' describes an extreme, eg: "This is too long." or "You are screaming too loud."

'Two' is a number.

Another common point of confusion relates to the difference between 'its' and 'it's.'

'Its' means 'belong to it', eg: "That is its case."

'It's' is an abbreviation for 'it is', eg: "It's stinky." Only use 'it's' when you could write 'it is' instead.

Distinguishing between 'then' and 'than' generally comes naturally to English speakers, but do you know the real meaning?

'Then' applies to time, eg: "Then I went out." 'Then' can also be used to mean 'in that case', eg: "If no-one is at the desk then you should ring for attention."

'Than' is used in making comparisons, eg: "This guide is better than that one."

Sometimes writers will mix up words that look similar and appear to have the same meanings – but they don't. Sometimes there is just a minor difference, but other times they have a totally different meaning.

Test yourself on these commonly confused words:

1. eminent/imminent
2. stationery/stationary
3. ensure/insure
4. complement/compliment
5. apprised/appraised
6. currently/presently
7. council/counsel

Look up any of these words that you are not sure of the meaning, and then make a habit of doing so in your daily writing activities. This will help you to make fewer mistakes and expand your vocabulary.

Personal Pronouns

Personal pronouns are the short words which are used to stand in for the full names of people and things, eg: 'I', 'him', 'she' and 'it'. Most of us use these words so often that we get them right without trying, but occasionally we might fall into this bad habit.

When listing a group of people who are doing something together, it is polite to put yourself last, eg: "Selena, Jeff and I are going to the movies." People often choose the wrong personal pronoun in this situation, eg: "Selena, Jeff and me are going to the movies." Because going [to the movies] is an active behavior, all of the people going are subjects in the sentence and should therefore take the nominative case. 'Me' is an accusative and dative form. In the opposite situation, you should not say "Selena gave the money to Jeff and I" but, rather, "Selena gave the money to Jeff and me" because, in that case, 'Jeff and me' are the indirect objects in the sentence.

Tip: imagine what the sentence would be like without the other person, eg: "Selena gave these documents to I." sounds obviously wrong.

Personal Pronouns and Gender

In business, you will not always know very much about the person you are addressing. Often, you will not know what sex that person is. When you are referring to an individual whose sex is unknown, you have several options available. Traditionally, the neutral personal pronoun in English has been the same as the masculine one, but this is becoming less common and can be considered rude.

The most popular neutral way to use third person singular pronouns in formal modern English is to write them as "he or she", "him or her", "Sir or Madam", etc. This method can make documents quite a bit longer, but is unlikely to attract disapproval.

The last option is less formal and even considered slang in some instances; however, it is the method I personally use most of the time. You can use the third person plural pronoun ('them', 'they', 'their') as an alternative to "he or she."

Whichever option you use, it is important to be consistent. Certainly, you should try to avoid changing pronouns within a single document. In some instances, it may be advisable to select the pronoun option which is most appropriate for a particular set of readers.

Titles

Many women are sensitive about the titles by which they are referred to - 'Mrs.', 'Miss' or 'Ms.' In some instances you may know that the addressee is female, but not know her title. In these cases, 'Ms' is the safer option, since it will not cause offense by making assumptions about marital status, but it is sometimes perceived as overly formal or as indicative of a political agenda.

Where an addressee's title is 'Dr.', 'Prof.', 'Rev', or similar, you can usually expect to be forgiven for not knowing.

The Sentence

In business writing your sentences must be grammatically correct and powerful. They must express your message clearly, concisely, and with no room for misunderstanding.

There are two purposes of sentences, to ask something or to tell something. To create an effective sentence, follow these guidelines:

1. Write in an active voice – Using active voice means constructing sentences where the subject acts. Here are a few samples:

> I kicked the ball.
> You are watching too much TV.
> Dave will watch a movie Friday evening.

In each of these sentences, the subject (I, You, and Dave respectively) performs the action of the verb (kicked, watching, will watch). Writing in the passive voice means constructing sentences where the subject is acted upon, rather than agents of the action.

2. Make your verbs powerful – Your verbs can energize your statements. An action verb generates more drama and emotion than a noun, adjective or adverb of similar meaning. Compare the following:

The children wept when their dog died. (strong verbs: wept, died)
The children shed tears over the death of their dog. (nouns: tears, death)
The children were sad when their dog was dead. (adjectives: sad, dead)

Use vivid verbs, powerful verbs, to fizz up the action, paint word-pictures, and create feelings in your readers.

3. Be specific by using specific words – Do not make the reader interpret your message. Many letters contain words and phrases such as report, document, handle, fix, and deal with. Each one of these can be understood in different ways, depending on context. It

is not your reader's job to figure out what you mean, but your job to make sure your message is clear.

4. Don't ramble – Stay focused on your message.

A Paragraph, the Unit of Thought

People often wonder how many sentences should be in a paragraph. There is no answer to that question. What counts is the way you put your sentences together. Think of a paragraph as a unit of thought, one though, one paragraph.

The first sentence in a paragraph should be the introductory sentence, telling the reader what this paragraph is going to be about. The middle sentences are the main content, and support what was stated in the introductory sentence. The last sentence in a paragraph, the concluding sentence, should bring the main content to a close.

Formatting Business Letters

No matter how trivial its content may be, the business letter is always of great importance. It often represents the first contact that a client will have with you, so it has to represent you well.

A standard business letter is a simple document to produce, and you should always try to produce your letters to the same format, even where your individual style may differ from others.

Your company header — usually your logo and a short slogan or description of what you do — should appear at the top of your letter, usually in the center or to the left. At the very bottom of your letter, ideally in a smaller typeface, you should include your company information – name, office address, telephone number, etc.. Some companies like to include an e-mail address and/or website URL in this position, but this may not be well suited to companies wanting to present a traditional image.

All pages should be clearly numbered. Ideally, you should number your pages as 'page 1 of 2', etc., so that readers can be sure they are not missing any parts of a longer letter.

The main body of text in a letter should be written in a plain, clear font, and an easily legible size. Most businesses prefer to align text at the left margin, as when writing by hand or using a typewriter, but some, especially those working in design or aiming for a modern image, choose to justify text. When text is justified, a word processor adjusts the spacing between letters so that all lines appear to be of the same length, and the left and right margins are both even.

At the top of a letter, at the left hand side, you should write your name, your company name, and the address where you can be contacted (provided this information is not contained in your header). You may also wish to include a telephone number so that it is prominent and easy for the reader to find.

Beneath this information, you should leave a blank line, and then you should write the date on which the letter is being written. Some businesses prefer to write this out in full, to give a more elegant impression.

Underneath the date you should leave a blank line, and beneath that you should write the name and address of the person to whom your letter is addressed. Whenever possible, you should always address your letter to a person rather than directly to an organization. If you cannot find out the name of the appropriate person, you can address your letter by business title, eg: 'The Engineering Director.'

Underneath all this information, you should leave a blank line and then begin your letter. At the end of your letter, you should close (on a new line) with 'yours sincerely' or 'sincerely'; there are other variations on this, and it is possible to be creative, but these are the only two you really need for business writing. You should leave a few blank lines underneath this and then type your name. After you have printed the letter, you will want to sign your name by hand in the blank space.

Some business people who have to sign a lot of letters prefer to print their signatures, usually as images, or fill them in with a stamp. You can do this if you wish, however, it may affect the legal standing of your letter, since it would be possible for someone else to forge your signature by this means. A hand-written ink signature conveys a better impression. It shows that you have gone to the trouble to be personally involved with the letter, even if an assistant has actually written it.

Where more than one signature is required at the end of a letter, for instance, where it is from all the directors of a company, blank spaces should be left for each in turn, with their names printed beneath. The most senior should sign first.

Writing Memos

Memo is short for Memorandum. You can use either term, depending on how formal a tone you want. Use memos for communicating inside your company only. Information about meeting schedules, reorganizations, announcements, and changes in procedure are usually conveyed with memos.

Always use the standard memo format, unless your company has a specific format. If you follow the format, recipients will know exactly where to find the memos main purpose, call to actions, and other information.

Standard Memo Format:

Date:

To:

From:

Subject:

[memo body]

Memos are generally short, with one to four sentences. A longer format might have several paragraphs but should never be longer than one page. Your subject line should explain simply and clearly what the memo is about. The body can contain up to three parts. The opening part of the body – the first sentence or two – should give the main point of the memo. The middle part of the body should give instruction or information, such as, explain the problem or policy. The conclusion of the memo – the last few sentences – you can reaffirm or summarize the memo or call something to action, such as, request feedback. A memo does not require a salutation, but it is acceptable to put one.

Writing Email

Email is now widely being used in the business world. Email etiquette is important for communicating more effectively and efficiently with others. Emails are usually short and concise. Even though email is less formal than a business letter, your emails still need to be written in a professional manner – applying all of the principles we have already covered.

Here are some things to keep in mind the next time you sit down to write an email:

1. Use an appropriate subject– You need to have a subject line that is meaningful and to the point if you want the email to get read. There are just too many emails competing for attention, so using a generic subject, such as, 'Hi,' might be ignored by the reader or sent down to the bottom of the inbox.
2. Get to the point – Emails are not the place for writing a novel. Be respectful of other people's time by being as brief and as concise as possible.
3. Do not type in all capital letters – Writing in all capitals comes across as shouting. Not only is it annoying, but it is hard on the eyes and difficult to read.

This page is intentionally left blank

Example
Memos, Letters, and Emails

MEMORANDUM

Date: September 30, 2006

From: Fredric Hornblower

To: All Research Staff

Subject: Commendation – Teddy Bear – Space Demand Project

The purpose of this is to officially commend Teddy Bear for his exceptional contribution throughout his assignment to the Space Demand Project.

As you know, Teddy has been working on special assignment with the Space Demand team for the past eight months. Now that he is about to return to your part of the organization I wanted to make sure that he gets some recognition for his significant and exceptional contributions to the project.

As a PM, Teddy's role in the project was pivotal to its timely and successful completion. It was Teddy who worked long hours, numerous nights and weekends with his small team of researchers, first specifying, and then testing the thousands of equations that had to be run. The quality of Teddy's written work was also exceptional. His regression analysis summaries were always very well written and rarely required revision.

In closing, I would like to say that I have worked with research PMs over the years and have never run across one as professional and productive as Teddy Bear was on this project. I believe that the organization as a whole should recognize his exceptional contribution to a major project.

Please let me know if you have any questions or comments.

Fredric Hornblower
Research Director

MEMO

Date: August 12, 2003

From: Management

To: All Employees

Subject: Meeting Reminder

This is to remind all employees of the meeting with MeetUs Corporation on August 26, 2003 at 4 PM. The meeting will take place in Bells Conference room. Please arrive early.

Please let me know if you have any questions or comments.

Management

November 18, 2006

Mr. Raymond Fielding
President
SpaceShip
1850 Highridge Road
Columbus, Ohio 43201

Dear Raymond:

Riverview Development is pleased to submit our letter of interest to participate in your development project.

Since being invited to address this exciting opportunity, our team members have collaborated to produce a preliminary plan that we believe will energize the public, strengthen the space exploration, and produce long-term benefits for the entire space program.

As you know, we are a team of professionals with a proven track record in this discipline that has the ability to successfully transform our plan into reality. Our team is comprised of members who have worked together on numerous successful projects. They have been assembled for this project because of the enormous trust and confidence they have in one another. You can be assured that the lead partners in our group will manage the project closely and carefully, and accountability for results will never be delegated.

In the weeks ahead, we look forward to receiving comments from SpaceShip and the steering committee about our preliminary. We understand that right now the plan is clearly a 'work in progress' which can only be improved by input from the various stakeholders who care the most about the project. We therefore look forward to using their input to develop a comprehensive integrated final development plan.

Thank you for giving us the opportunity to participate.

Sincerely,

Brad Tyler
President

Ray Mache
Manager, Corporate Programs
Fast Publications
456 Faulkner Dr
Clearfield, UT 84015

July 22, 2008

Ms. Hannah Gomez
Director, Corporate Services
XYZ Industries
245 Dearborn Park Road
Chicago, Il 60610

Dear Ms. Gomez:

It was a pleasure meeting you briefly at the chamber of commerce meeting last week. I was fascinated by your synopsis of the history of XYZ Industries over the past, almost half-century. Clearly, your company has a rich corporate heritage and tradition. At the same time, the company has been blessed with a continuum of leaders of foresight and imagination who had the courage to change course at key points along the way so that the company could remain competitive and continue to lead its industry.

As I was mentioning to you, Fast Publications is a specialty publisher that focuses on corporate publications including annual reports, corporate profiles and corporate histories. We have been in business for over 5 years and during that time have grown from a one-man start-up, to a serious corporate publisher with over 50 employees. We have been contracted by over a dozen Fortune 500 companies to produce both annual and special occasion publications on their behalf.

After our chat at last week's meeting, it occurred to me that with XYZ Industries approaching its 25th anniversary, it would be the perfect occasion to produce a Corporate History to celebrate your company's first quarter-century. It so happens, that these are exactly the types of corporate publications that we specialize in here at Fast Publications. In fact, we have produced corporate histories for a number of companies.

With XYZ Industries 25th just around the corner, I'm sure that you have been thinking about ways to make that anniversary a special one. Accordingly, I would very much like to meet with you and show you some of the corporate work we have done, and brief you further on our services. I have a strong feeling that what we offer at Fast Publications might be just the kind of thing you've been looking for to celebrate XYZ Industries 25th.

Please feel free to call me at 405-745-2358 so that we can discuss this further. If I don't hear from you by the end of next week I will follow up with you and see if we can set up a meeting at your convenience.

Yours truly,

Ray Mache
Manager, Corporate Programs

To: homer@foxed.com
From: bart.stimpson@flanders.org
Subject: Investment Idea

Homer,

I have seen a number of investment (and scams) ideas during my last trip to Utah. I'd like to share one with you that I'm seriously thinking of getting involved with that just may strike your fancy.

I don't know if you would be interested in a patent protected, brushless direct current motor or not. Brushless direct current motors offer the possibility of replacing the current motor or generators that are used in a large variety of applications including electric cars and wind turbines. As an example, GE recently bought a Swedish company to get this type of technology.

In case you are also interested, I look forward to your comments.

Sincerely,

Bart Stimpson

To: xyzperson@abccompany.org
From: cap@psued.edu
Subject: Application for summer internship

Dear Ms. Clinton,

I am writing in response to the ad posted on gobignow.net for a summer information systems/technology internship at Centurion Financial. Please accept my attached resume and letter as an application for this position. My skills and experience closely fit the posted job description, and I hope to hear from you soon.

Thank you,

Barak Bush

Section 2

Presenting and Public Speaking

Not so long ago only managers and executives made business presentations. Now the corporate specialty of presentations has infiltrated every possible level in every organization. Today people at all levels are expected to be able to present their ideas and plans competently and positively to various audiences both inside and outside of the organization.

Here are the five key things you should think about when creating a presentation:

1. Know the subject
2. Know your audience
3. Set your objective
4. Plan, plan, and plan
5. Open and close with a bang

> Every presentation is an opportunity to advance your career.

Know the Subject

Knowing the subject inside and out is the most important thing when presenting. It is very easy for me to make a presentation on a subject that I have an extensive knowledge of; whereas, subjects I am not familiar with, I will not be able to put together the same quality presentation. Thoroughly study the subject and information regarding your presentation if you are not completely familiar with it. During the presentation you want to be the expert. You need to feel that you can properly answer any questions asked. Having the necessary knowledge and being the expert on the presentation topic will help reduce your tension and increase your confidence.

Your audience will be more engaged in the presentation if you use personal stories and everyday examples to help them relate to your subject. Here are a few suggestions to think about as you are creating your presentation:

- Use comfortable language, words, and phrases that both you and the audience will know.
- Share brief stories that help make your point.
- Provide examples that help the audience relate.

- Ask the audience questions to engage them in your subject or to see how much they already know.

Know the Audience

It is important to know who will be in the audience to hear your presentation. You would present a topic differently to a group of second graders than you would to a group of

> Every time you stand up to give a presentation you are selling, whether you are actually selling a product or service, or just your ideas and skills.

IRS workers, so knowing who will make up your audience is very important to know before you start to prepare. Find out as much as you can about the audience to help tailor your message. Here are some questions regarding the audience you might want to know the answer to before you begin to plan:

- Who will make up the audience?
- Why are they in attendance?
- What do they want to get out of the event?
- What do they know about my topic?
- What is their level of interest in my topic?
- Why are they interested in my topic?
- What will they do with the information?
- Will they be thinking about or engaged in something else while I am speaking?
- Are they being forced to be there and would rather be anywhere else but there?

Setting Your Objective

In order to create an effective presentation, you must be clear about your objective. First, ask yourself why you are giving the presentation? What is the purpose of the presentation? What do I want the audience to know or understand about the presentation? What do I want the audience to do at the end of the presentation? The answers to these questions are so important that I recommend you begin planning your presentation by writing the following words on a note card:

At the end of my presentation, I want . . . [then state your objective]

Then complete the statement as specifically and completely as possible. Here is an example of a good objective:

> "At the end of this presentation, I want the committee to approve my plan to sell tech-widgets by the fourth quarter of this year."

Notice that this objective is not only specific, but measurable. The committee will either approve the plan or not. It is not always possible to have such a measurable objective, but try to be as specific as possible. An appropriate objective will help you select the material to include in the presentation, and stop you from taking the presentation off on tangents.

Each person is going to bring their own expectation to your presentation. For the most part, you cannot control their expectations, but you need to be very clear about your own expectations. If you do not know what you want your presentation to achieve, then you cannot effectively prepare or present.

Pre-Presentation Strategy

There are a few things you can do before your presentation to help you achieve your objective.

> If you don't know where you are going, how will you know when you are there? An effective presentation requires a roadmap.

For example, if you think your presentation is going to be controversial, it is a good idea to make sure someone in the audience will be on your side. Also you might want someone in the audience to verbally backup or confirm one of your main points. You might also want to figure out which individuals will be the least persuaded by your presentation and prepare to backup your viewpoints in a way specific to that individual.

Another thing to consider is what kind of thinkers your audience will be. If your audience is largely financial types, your presentation should concentrate on facts and logical arguments. Such people generally want to hear all of the details. Be ready with a handout to provide any backup information that you did not include in your presentation. If you have mainly salespeople as your audience, you might want to make your points emotional while presenting fewer facts.

Plan Your Format

A common reason for failed presentations is caused by poor organization. Often presenters are tempted to include everything they know about the subject in their presentation, which can make it difficult to organize. This can overwhelm the presenter. Furthermore, too much information will also overwhelm the audience and cause them to simply stop listening.

> A logical format makes it easier for you to present and easier for the audience to understand.

Choose what information to include in your presentation, what to include in the form of a handout, and what information to leave out altogether. It helps to refer to your written objective during this process. For each section of your presentation, ask yourself if this information will help accomplish your objective, if not, take it out.

Three Styles to Format your Presentation:

Problem/solution

This is the most interesting and effective presentation format. Identify a problem, and then describe it in terms that point out the breadth and depth of the issue. Now dazzle the audience with your solution. This is similar to diet ads, where they show a horrible before picture, and then show a great after picture. You can use this same ploy in your presentation.

Topical

If you must have a number of unrelated topics in a single presentation, then a topical presentation is the best format to use. Using good transition between each topic will allow the audience to easily follow.

Sometimes you might want to find a common theme in all of the topics so it feels they are all related.

Chronological

This format is best suited when you must cover some history to illustrate your message.

Speaking

Confident speaking is a hallmark of the successful professional. Effective public speaking begins the moment the presenter walks on stage or steps behind the podium or stands in front of a group. Body language and appropriate dress give the first impression of a speaker to an audience. Being well groomed and using confident body language, with tall posture and eye contact, sends a message that the speaker is someone that the audience should listen to.

> Tell them what you're going to tell them, tell them, then tell them what you told them.

Your Opening

This is the decisive moment of your presentation. You must grab your audience's attention in the first few moments of your presentation. You must capture their attention and give them a reason to listen to you. Your audience may be required to be there physically, but mentally they can leave at any time. One of the best ways to get the audiences initial attention is to wow them with a powerful statement or question. Also avoid starting in a predictable fashion.

Here is a good example:

> "We have all gathered here to attend the condolence meeting of our company that has ceased operations yesterday."

Would that get your attention? No doubt, this will grab the audience's attention, but just be careful not to go over the top. From there you can provide more available information depending on your audience and objective. After you successfully grab the audience's attention, immediately move into the body of your presentation.

> TIP: A good trick is to write out the first few minutes of your presentation. Try to write it in spoken form, using contractions like, can't or won't, this will make it sound natural. Then memorize it word-for-word, this will help reduce nervousness and help you make good initial eye contact.

Close with a Bang

You want to make sure that your presentation has a lasting impact on your audience's mind. The end of your presentation should address whatever it was you wanted your audience to take from your presentation. Reviewing your key points can bring any presentation to a successful close. Always remember that this should be a summary and not a repetition of all the details. You may also want to end your presentation by seeking immediate action, such as asking for approval.

Practice Five Minutes at a Time

Practice the presentation in small chunks of time. Pull out the note cards and practice just one section at a time. For example, practicing the introduction for a few minutes, several times a day, will embed that part of the speech in your mind. This will create confidence and smoothness. If this rehearsal method is followed for the entire speech, the note cards will only be needed as a backup in the case you get nervous or forget.

Get the Audience to Participate

Here are some ideas how to increase the audience's participation and enhance their presentation experience:

- Use humor – this is the best way of keeping an audience lively, interested, and receptive.

- Ask for input – request a poll, a show of hands, or getting an audience member to share in the experience with you.

- Share a quote – a good quote can focus your audience's attention.

- Use props – do something unexpected, if it is appropriate. Seed the audience with people who will feed correct answers or achieve something to provide surprise. Use as many props as are needed to create a lively environment

- Ask open questions – try to bring an audience along, rather than dictating to them. Ask open questions and genuinely be receptive to the answers. Allow the audience input to sway the direction of the presentation if this is possible.

Use Transitions to Help Keep the Audience Engaged

Audiences stay engaged when they are actively involved as you are speaking. Transitions can accomplish this, by requiring some sort of action or response from the audience. Transitions can be words or actions. Examples of simple transitions are:

- Moving from one side of the stage to another. (The audience must follow the speaker with their eyes.

- Having members of the audience turn to the person next to them and discuss something

- Bringing out a visual aid

- Switching a prop

- Doing something unexpected, such as raising or lowering the tone of voice

- Having the audience members perform an action or small task

Respect the Audience

It is important for a speaker to respect the audience. Beginning and finishing the presentation on time shows respect for their busy schedules. Speaking to the audience's level of expertise shows respect for their knowledge. Being well groomed and well mannered shows respect to their sensibilities.

Public speaking does not have to be a fearful proposition. In fact, well-prepared presenters often feel that it is enjoyable. These tips will help reduce fear, build confidence, and develop effective professional public speaking skills.

Pauses

There are two types of pauses that you can use as you are speaking. These pauses can help you effectively convey your message.

Short

Short pauses will last from one to two seconds; they are for the simple purpose of separating your thoughts. This gives your audience a chance to catch up and absorb what you just said. Changing the tone of your voice slightly at the end of each thought will let the audience know you are moving into a new thought. Also, use a short pause before and after any phrase or word you want to emphasize.

Long

Pauses lasting more than two seconds can be very powerful, but they must be used correctly. These longer pauses give the audience a time to think about what you just said, that is if what you just said was worth thinking about. Using long pauses un-effectively will ruin your presentation, so be careful.

Movement and Hand Gestures

Proper movement can add a lot of power to your words. The last thing you want to do is to stand up and look like a statue during your presentation. Movement can help you connect with the audience and help you to look more comfortable and natural.

Smaller movements, such as, taking a few steps or shifting your body's direction, can be used as a great transition from one thought to another. As you make this kind of movement you want to add a pause in your speech.

Larger movement must always have a clear purpose. If you are talking about or to a specific individual, then you can walk over to them. If you want to point something out on the screen, then you can walk up to the screen and point it out. You can also move around the stage as need. If you want the audience to be focused on you, then move to the front center of the stage. If you want the audience to think about what you are saying you will want to move off to one of the sides.

Hand gestures can help you look more natural, but you do want to keep them to a minimum. Let your hand gestures follow your words. If you say "1," then hold up one finger, if you say "2," then hold up two fingers, or if you are talking about something specific in the room, point at it. Just make sure your hand gestures go with what you are saying.

One thing to avoid is physical ticks, these are unrelated gestures that use to often. Many people will grasp their hands together and then throw them up and apart for each point that they make. You need to look for what ticks you have and try to avoid using them in your presentation.

Visual Aids

The purpose of visual aids is to 'aid' your presentation, not be your presentation. Too often presenters underestimate the importance of visual aids and their presentations suffer. They spend most of the time thinking about what they will say, and then visual aids are an afterthought.

Visual aids help you to gain and then keep an audience's attention, and help reinforce your message. Effective visuals can double the impact of your presentation. People are less likely to misunderstand what you are telling them, if they can both see and hear your message. Furthermore, information conveyed by more than one means is more likely to be remembered longer.

Choosing Visual Aids

There are many different options available for visual aids. It is important to select the visual aids that are most appropriate for your occasion. The types of visual aids in which you choose should depend on a number of factors, which might include your audience, the size of your audience, the particular room the presentation will be held in, and what type of material you are presenting.

Types of Visual Aids

- Objects: Things that are tangible, for example, animals, books, model replicas, globes, or a person.

- Photographs: Photographs work best if enlarged or presented in a computer slideshow.

- Flip Charts, Whiteboards, and Chalkboards: Most often used in classroom settings or board meetings and work well for presenting key points as a presentation progresses.

- Drawings: Includes not only sketches but also maps, diagrams, and graphs.

- Charts: Best used to summarize large amounts of information.

- Videotapes, Slides, and DVDs: Especially effective when demonstrating a process or explaining a place or event.

- Multimedia Presentations: two or more types of visuals aids wrapped up into one, which allow speakers to provide a wide range of material during the course of a presentation.

Choose your form of visual aids based on its appropriateness for the situation, as well as your own level of comfort in using that form.

A Common Presentation Mistake

Here is a common scenario of a bad business presenter. The company CFO must make a presentation to the Board of Directors on the financial outlook. The CFO loathes giving these presentations so much, he waits to prepare until the last minute. He types up his speech word-for-word, and then prints out a copy for each person attending. As an afterthought, he prints an extra copy as an overhead transparency; this will be his visual aid.

I feel sorry for the audience who must sit through this type of presentation. The presenter puts up a slide completely full of words. Often the

> Masses of words or figures are not visual aids.

audience cannot even read it, but that does not matter because the presenter then turns around, facing the screen and reads the slide aloud. Then, just in case you miss a word, you can refer to the handouts, which are exact copies of the slides. When I am in attendance of presentations where this happens, I feel insulted. You have to ask yourself why the presentation was needed at all, when a memo would have accomplished the same objective.

Visual Aids and Handouts are not the Same Thing

The best visual aids contain just enough information to support what you plan to say. Handouts are given to provide complete information on your presentation, or serve as reminders for later use.

> Visual aids contain skeleton information, while handouts give all of the details. They are not interchangeable.

If you are discussing financial information, you would want to use charts and graphs as visuals aids, instead of using large tables filled with numbers. At the end, you could then provide a handout with a complete set of financial statements. Wait until the end of your presentation to distribute the handout. If you pass it out at the beginning of your presentation, the audience will focus on studying the handout rather than listening to your presentation. Just let them know they will receive complete information at the end.

Sometimes I am asked to provide my set of slides before the

presentation, so they can be printed out and inserted into a booklet for the audience. If you created your presentation effectively then your slides should only contain the skeleton information. They will not contain enough information in them to be useful as a handout.

Tips for Presenting Visual Aids

Although the choice of visual aids is important, how those aids are used is even more important. After all, a speaker can have phenomenal visual aids, but if they are not displayed properly, discussed clearly and effectively, and integrated smoothly into the presentation, they will be of little or no value.

In order to get the maximum impact with visual aids:

- Talk to the audience, not to the PowerPoint slideshow, the flipchart, or the whiteboard.

- Avoid passing objects, photographs, handouts, etc., around among audience members during the presentation.

- When displaying an object, place it where everyone can see it; and display it only when discussing it.

- Clearly and concisely explain the information contained on any visual aid. Don't assume the audience will make the connection between the visual aid and your presentation.

- Practice using visual aids in advance of the actual presentation. In fact, speakers should rehearse the entire presentation, from start to finish, so they will be able to integrate visual aids smoothly, easily, and professionally.

This page is intentionally left blank

Section 3

Listening

"We have two ears and one mouth so that we can listen twice as much as we speak." - *Epictetus (Greek philosopher)*

Just because someone hears another person's words does not mean that they are really listening or comprehending what that person is saying. There is, after all, a big difference between hearing and listening.

The Difference between Hearing and Listening

Technically, hearing is the sensation produced by sound waves vibrating on the eardrums and the simultaneous firing of electrochemical impulses in the brain. Listening, on the other hand, involves not only paying close attention to what is heard but also comprehending the meaning of that sound.

When someone else is speaking you should be silent and focusing on what is being said. You should not be going over your reply in your mind and waiting for the other person to finish so that you can jump in, this is not listening. Listening is a conscious act, and we must practice it actively and consciously to be able to communicate effectively.

The Importance of Being a Good Listener

In most companies, effective listeners are not only more likely to be promoted but also, upon promotion, are more likely to obtain influential positions. Many business leaders will rate good listening skills as one of the most important skills to have. Further studies have been done discovering that college students with good listening skills have higher grade point averages (GPA), than those without.

The Causes of Poor Listening

While there are sometimes other contributing factors to poor listening, here are the four main causes:

1. Failure to concentrate – The average person talks at a rate of 120 to 150 words per minute, but the human brain can process an amazing 400 to 800 words per minute, causing people to experience "spare brain time," during which they are thinking about other things instead focusing on the speaker.

2. Concentrating too hard – Some people try to soak up everything a speaker is saying, which often causes them to miss the point, because it becomes lost in unimportant details.

3. Forming precipitous conclusions – People do this in two ways: either by thinking they know what the speaker is going to say and draw to the wrong conclusion; or they reject someone's ideas, before the person has even fully expressed their ideas.

4. Concentrating on manner of speaking and personal appearance – People focus their attention on how someone speaks, for example, accent, speech patterns, or even speech defects, or they focus their attention on someone's appearance, for example, facial features, dress attire, or hairstyle. As a result, they fail to concentrate upon what is actually being said.

Steps to Becoming a Better Listener

Becoming a better listener is not a passive process, which means you need to put effort into becoming better. There are several things you can do to help improve your listening skills:

- Resist distractions when listening – It is easy for you to be distracted by not only your own thoughts, but also external factors, for example, nearby conversations, cell phones ringing, a room that is too hot or too cold, crying babies, etc. As a result, you must make a conscious effort to keep your attention focused on the speaker.

- Avoid focusing on manner of speaking or appearance – You should never judge another person's ideas based upon how that person talks or looks. Just because someone is physically attractive and articulate, does not mean their ideas are any more valuable or valid than those of someone less physically attractive or less articulate.

- Do not jump to conclusions – You should hear out someone and allow them to finish speaking before deciding that person's ideas are misguided or foolish.

- Learn to focus on content – You need to listen for and concentrate on the main points begin conveyed and not make the mistake of reading between the lines and thinking you already know what that person will say.

It is possible for poor listeners to become good listeners. In order to improve your listening skills, you must actually want to become a better listener. After all, only then will you take the necessary steps to achieve this worthwhile goal.

Selective Listening

Someone starts talking and we assume we already know what they are going to say, so we jump to the end in our minds and stop listening. Not only can we easily receive the wrong information, but also offend the speaker. Focus on what is being said, as they are saying it, and let the message lead itself.

> "Examine what is said, not who speaks"
> - Arabian Proverb

A common cause of selective listening is personal bias against the speaker. It is natural to ignore or discredit the opinions of those we do not like. If someone start talking and you immediately switch off because you do not like that person, you are guilty of selective listening. Try to overcome this, just because you do not like the person, does not mean the information is not valid or useful.

Listen in Context

An attribute of the expert listener is the ability to hear the message that was not said. Every sentence fits into context with the surrounding information. Without the surrounding

> Understand the context is essential to understanding the message.

information, individual sentences may not make any sense or have a completely different meaning. For example, if you asked a child to run to the store to purchase something, and they replied, "It's raining outside," you would understand that they are using the weather as a reason not to go to the store. On the other hand, someone looking out of the window in the morning may make the same comment simply as a fact, but not relating to anything in particular.

Understanding the context helps keep the discussion on track. As an example, in a meeting the marketing director suggests a promotional event as part of a new product launch. As background, he talks about a block party that took place in his neighborhood to raise awareness of neighborhood crime. One associate responded by doubting the appropriateness of a block party for this particular product, while another begins to complain about the local police. In this example, the effective listener realized the context, and responded about the director's idea for a promotional event. Effective listeners will be able to recognize the difference between the main point of the statement and the illustrative example.

Listen for Facts, Not Opinions

Facts can be distorted with biased words and expressions. Sometimes people have a lot invested in their opinions that they make statements based off of hope, rather than fact. Here is an example, "This new process will revolutionize the way our company operates!" This statement may be true, but it may not be the kind of revolution you want, or it may not be true at all.

To be an effective listener you must learn to decide what information is fact and what is just someone's opinion. People color their words in many different ways, adding to the challenge of listening. Learn to strip away the opinion and propaganda, and listen for the facts.

Active Listening

Sometimes speakers leave gaps in the information they are presenting. An effective active listener will be able to help guide the speaker and allow them to fill in the missing information.

Often a speaker needs the opportunity to restate what they have said to be understood. You can provide them this opportunity by asking them to clarify what they just said. That is why listening sometimes involves speaking.

The Art of Questioning

Part of your job when actively listening is to help the speaker convey their thoughts. You can ask strategic questions to help guide the speaker and fill in the gaps in their message. There are two types of questions, closed and open. Closed questions would be answered with a yes or no, whereas open questions require information to answer them.

> Questioning is an important and helpful aspect of listening.

Typically you would use a closed question for confirmation and open questions to receive specific information, broaden the conversation, or to direct the conversation.

Broadening

These questions require a detailed response that will bring in more information and broaden the discussion.

"Megan, you've provided us information about the new technology they are using at Super Corporation and it appears to be exciting. How do you think we can start to develop similar technology?"

Clarifying or Confirming

When you ask these types of questions, you allow the speaker to provide clarification of their point.

"Are you saying you agree with David's suggestion?"

"So, you believe that tech-widgets are profitable?"

Questioning Example

Here is an example that makes use of all the different questioning techniques:

Listener: How is information received inside the company?

Speaker: Newsletters, staff meetings, memos, and emails.

Listener: How do you find these communications helpful?

Speaker: We use them primarily to keep the company informed and unified.

Listener: Give me an example of that?

Speaker: Last month we announced our new product line in the newsletter and then used the staff meeting as an opportunity for the staff to ask questions about it.

Listener: Do you think the combination of both of the newsletter and staff meeting worked well in this instance?

> The right questions can help you fill in gaps in the speaker's message

Speaker: Yes.

Working with Emotions

When people are angry or upset, an effective listener will work to subdue those negative emotions before they begin to solve the problem. A great example of this is when a child falls and scrapes their knees. The mother will first comfort the child with a hug before addressing the wound. Business professionals can benefit from this same process.

A frustrated and angry customer or client will want you to recognize their emotions before moving on to corrective actions. If you first respond to their complaint by asking for identifying information, such as name or address, the customer will remain angered, making it more difficult to solve the problem. First you want to defuse their anger or frustration by showing them you understand by saying something such as, "I am sorry to hear that, I can understand why this problem is causing you frustration." Defusing the emotions first often goes a long way to correcting the problem.

You also need to listen to yourself, so that you can recognize and deal with your own emotional responses. We all have 'buttons' – attitudes and feelings that make us respond emotionally when people bring up certain topics or express particular opinions. It is important to be aware of them so that you can decide how to react, rather than be controlled by your own emotions.

Depending on various facts—the subject under discussion, the identity of the person who has upset you, the purpose of the conversation—you might choose one of three options:

- Ignore the comment and move on.
- Speak your opinion on the comment, and then continue the conversation on the original track.
- Mention it and make an issue of the remark.

There are occasions where each one is appropriate. Keep in mind the moment you lose control of your emotions, effective communication will be lost.

Acknowledgement the Speaker

You can acknowledge someone by using a verbal or nonverbal response. A nonverbal acknowledgement might be a simple nod of the head, a smile, or raising an eyebrow. These signs let the speaker know that you are paying attention.

For verbal acknowledgements you can inject phrases such as, "I understand," "Really?," and "that's Interesting." These phrases indicate that you understanding what is being said, and lets the speaker know you are paying attention. Furthermore, acknowledgments help increase your relationship with the speaker.

Need help improving your communication skills?

Arrow College teaches an online certificate course using this book.

Course Description

The online course is designed for people who want to improve their professional communication skills.

The course will cover how to effectively write powerful letters, memos, reports, and e-mails. Business writing is often the main line of communication inside and outside of any company, making writings skills important to master.

Not so long ago only managers and executives made business presentations. Today people at all levels are expected to be able to present their ideas and plans competently and positively to various audiences both inside and outside of the organization. We will arm you with the knowledge required to make a powerful presentation. We believe that every time you give a presentation, it is an opportunity to advance your career.

The course will cover:

- WRITING
- SPEAKING
- PRESENTING
- LISTENING

Enroll today at http://arrowcollege.org

About the Author

Bracken Meyers is a business and engineering professional. He is currently the CEO and President of Centurion Financial, serves on the board of directors of The Technical Management Institute, and is a research and development consultant.

He has many published works on writing, planning, leadership, alternative energy, and technical papers. He also has many years of experience in giving technical presentations. He opened his first business, Fire Charged Web Hosting, at the age of 16. He has a "can do" attitude, and brings success and sensibility everywhere he goes.

Acknowledgments

I would like to thank the following individual for helping with the editing and proof reading:

Cheryl Meyers

Heather Gentry

Loretta Borger

Notes

Notes

Notes

Notes

Notes

Notes

www.ingramcontent.com/pod-product-compliance
Lightning Source LLC
Chambersburg PA
CBHW051243170526
45165CB00004B/1550